Single, $uccessful and Sleepy

GERMAINE MOODY

Foreword by Brian T. Shirley

Become Endless Publishing

Single, $uccessful and Sleepy, by Germaine Moody.

© 2014 Become Endless Publishing.
All rights reserved. Printed in the United States of America.
No part of this book may be used or reproduced in any manner
whatsoever without written permission except in the case of
brief quotations embodied in critical articles and reviews.

For information, address:
Become Endless Publishing, 4322 N. Kenmore Ave Suite 4L,
Chicago, IL 60613

Or email becomeendlesspublishing@gmail.com.

ISBN-10: 0692294112
ISBN-13: 978-0692294116

To all of those, past and present, all races, cultures and nationalities, around the world, who have come before me so that I'm now able to do what I do, freely, and creatively, to uplift, to motivate, to inspire and to bring people together, I thank you for your life, your vision, your genius, your ideas, your sacrifice, the hard work you have invested and the greatness you have shared. I and others are now reaping a global return beyond our own understanding that we did not have to labor for, and because of that, this publication is dedicated to you.

Thank you Brian T. Shirley for joining me, not only are you an amazing comedian, you're also an amazing man with an amazing heart. A special thank you to my friends Torry Williams, Adrienne Noel and Stanley Nwobi for being a part of the three Q&A interviews included in the book. To my family, my destiny team and worldwide supporters, as always, Thank You for being a part of my journey of life.

-Germaine Moody

TO-DO LIST

1 THE FIRST DATE	1
2 FLIRTING: HARMLESS OR HAZARDOUS	5
3 THE LIARS THE BUYERS	9
4 GO FOR A WALK	13
5 KNOW YOUR TYPE	17
6 DON'T BE TOO AVAILABLE	21
7 BREAKFAST ANYONE	25
8 SINGLE BY CHOICE OR SINGLE BY NECESSITY	29
9 THE POWER OF SLEEP	33
10 DINNER ON ME	37
Q&A: TORRY WILLIAMS	41
11 THE NEW NORMAL	47

12 THE POWER OF COMMITMENT	51
13 LISTEN TO YOUR PEACE	55
14 TO TEXT OR NOT TO TEXT	59
15 THE AWKWARD THE UNEXPECTED THE UNPREDICTABLE	63
16 ROAD TRIP OF A LIFETIME	67
17 SOLITUDE VS. LONELINESS	71
18 CHILDREN OR NO CHILDREN	75
19 NOTHING ON TV CREATE YOUR OWN SHOW	79
20 THE PICKUP LINE VS. THE ELEVATOR PITCH	83
Q&A: ADRIENNE NOEL	87
21 SOCIAL MEDIA DO'S AND DON'TS	93
22 DEALING WITH A BROKEN HEART	99

23 UNANNOUNCED ENVY	103
24 MOVIE ANYONE	107
25 WILLING TO WAIT	111
26 ONLY SLEEP FOR REST OR DEATH	115
27 LOVE LIFE OR CHANGE IT	117
28 A NEW SEASON	121
29 WORK OUT AND WORK IT	125
30 THANK GOD FOR PETS	129
Q&A: STANLEY NWOBI	133
31 AGREE TO DISAGREE	139
32 WHAT ABOUT YOUR FRIENDS	143
33 I KNOW WHAT YOU DID LAST YEAR	147
34 ONLY STOP TO CHANGE DIRECTIONS	151

35 DON'T GET UPSET GET BACK TO LIFE	155
36 THIRTY-SIX HOURS A DAY EIGHT DAYS A WEEK	159
37 THE ALL-NIGHTER	163
38 THE POWER OF AN HEIR	167
39 SHARING THE KNOWLEDGE	171
40 THE POWER OF SUCCESS	175

Foreword

"Single, $uccessful and Sleepy" can best be summed up by the title of Day 27 "Love Life or Change It", that is if you want the very short version. This book will change your life from the inside out if you choose to follow Germaine's advice. Each topic takes us through a fresh new outlook one can have when it comes to romantic or professional life. The techniques discussed can be used to achieve success in both arenas and more!

Germaine has a knack for reaching into the reader's mind and answering the questions that form as you read this book. Does one have to be married to be successful? What about having a pet? How important is sleep, diet and exercise? Are all-nighters always bad? How easy or hard are changes to make? How big or small are the changes one needs to make to begin with?

Taking each section day by day can lead to a 40-day transformation in this devotional, but that's not the only benefit. Really learning and committing to what this book is about lends itself to being more than a self-help process. It's a new way to look at, enjoy, succeed and find what you desire in life.

To read and understand Germaine's timely and brilliant "Single, Successful & Sleepy" book is to discover your maximum potential as a business professional while approaching life and its unexpected personal challenges all at the same time.

Brian T. Shirley

Connect with Brian at http://about.me/brians.

DAY 1
THE FIRST DATE.

We all know how important the first date is, mainly because it could also be the last date. This can be quite similar to meeting a potential business partner or new professional contact. First impressions are, how shall I say it, very impressionable. In most cases we believe we have somewhat an idea of what to expect, besides, what all could go wrong on the first date right? Oh boy! Never ask that question because the universe will gladly show you what the possibilities are. Instead, why not just prepare for it? Seriously, any previous information or knowledge you have about the person or people you are meeting (personal or business), use that to your advantage. I'm not saying call their family members, high school, job, church, gym, local library, internet provider, the nearest McDonald's, landlord, mail man and next door neighbor to do a thorough investigation. Just do some basic research if you can, to give yourself the heads up but don't believe everything you read and hear though.

Knowledge is power, plus you can use some of the background information you researched as a conversation topic, but don't make it obvious that you've done a lot of research. This could turn out to be a promising relationship, business partnership or just a great friend for life. Make sure you've given them some insight into who you are also, so there's a better give and take in the conversation. There's nothing worse than a one-sided date. Who does that?!! I'm sure I have before but it's not cool at all. If you know you're not interested in the person or the business opportunity at the beginning, I don't recommend hanging around the entire time, unless you just want to be cordial or have nothing better to do. Me personally, I'm out of there! Life is short and sometimes people can't catch on to the signs and signals we make so obvious. A good friend and I often talk about carrying a red and white road "STOP" sign (without the pole) to restaurants, dates and meetings, so when someone is talking too much (waiter, the date or anyone around) or when we realize things aren't going as good as we want them to, we'd just hold up the "STOP" sign then proceed to switch routes and leave. I've learned that the longer you stay, the more the other person believes all is well. Don't lead anyone on, just be professional, end it and get out of there as fast as possible. People are very unpredictable these days so I suggest you run out! There will be another date soon, you're too amazing to not give it another try. Notice all the "STOP" signs today when you're out and about. Laugh a little. You never know, it might work on the next date. At least people do stop on the road when they see one, most of them.

DAY 2
FLIRTING: HARMLESS OR HAZARDOUS?

You know I have to address the topic of flirting somewhere in the book, we might as well do it now while we're all still in a good mood, some of us. To be safe and to keep spouses, boyfriends and girlfriends out of our face, let's look at flirting only from a single perspective when it comes to dating and business. If both individuals are single, flirting is probably the way to go, and it has great potential to end your singleness. It has to be balanced though, flirting with too many people will create a new reputation for you that your neighborhood and people at your job can't wait to talk about. There's a sense of flirting that goes on in business whether you've noticed it or desire to acknowledge it. We all want to be liked by our business partners, employers, co-workers, supervisors or employees. We want to appeal to our colleagues so they'll stick around and so they'll also want to keep us around. The goal is to define your own definition of flirting, as well as when to apply it for your advantage and when not to. It's often used as a form of persuasion in business circles, mostly to seal a business deal. Other times it's because someone is truly interested in you and sees this as a prime opportunity, so they attempt to take advantage of the situation. I'll be honest, I've done it before, several people have.

Some lunch meetings end up serving large entrées of Flirt Migeon and way too many glasses of Charm'donnay because flirting can also be unpredictable and hard to deny, especially if you're attracted to the individual. Sadly, people may perceive a compliment from another person as flirting, even when that person isn't remotely interested in them on that level, not even, no possibility, not thinking happily-ever-after, no way. Flirting can be harmless if used properly, but leave the mailman, UPS, and FedEx teams alone, I'm just saying, they have access to too many people already. It's true though, they can meet more people in a day than most singles meet in a year. Wait a minute, maybe I need to change careers.

Flirting can be hazardous as well because like I said, people are unpredictable. Best advice if you're going to flirt, let the other person flirt first, if you can hold out long enough. At least you'll know or can act like you know that they're interested. Now you just need to pray that they're single, all the way single. Beware, people have weird definitions of 'single' these days, I won't go there, yet. And to the married and attached people, leave us alone, stop flirting with us, it's hard enough as it is trying to decide between launching a new business, starting a new job, going back to school vs. entering a new relationship, it all seems like the same. We don't need anymore complications from you supposedly "happily married" people hitting on us. Use your instinct and discernment when flirting. You have the power to make it harmless or hazardous. Keep an eye out for "Professional Flirters", if you know what I mean, they're only out for one thing, from as many men and women that will hand it over. Hand them a "STOP" sign if one approaches you.

DAY 3
THE LIARS. THE BUYERS.

Being single and successful has its benefits, like not waking up to snoring all night every night, the remote control is always in place, being able to travel outside of your city, state or country to meet someone instead of settling for the locals and so on. Of course there are disadvantages as well. We should remain aware that there are those roaming around like stray animals willing and ready to bring destruction and a truck load of bull into your life at any given moment if allowed. They lie, they cheat, they cause emotional breakdowns, divorces, depression and more. Some people have nothing better to do than to prey on the successful, just to see what they can get out of them. They've made it into a career, seriously. I refer to these as "The Liars". They want us, they want us bad, like syrup on pancakes, that makes me hungry, hold on…

OK I'm back, like text messages to a teenager, like TMZ to a celebrity taking out the trash, like free Wifi to someone who doesn't have internet access, we are in demand. Whether it's personal or business, you can spot The Liars easily if you enhance your observation skills, stop winking your eye at the convenient store clerk and just pay attention. Listen and watch people carefully, notice any imbalance, oddness, multiple promises, over-the-top interest in you and bad timing in their words and actions. Businesses and corporations are in the same boat, they can be thrown into this category with their false advertisements, over promising benefits of a product and treating employees like third class passengers on the Titanic. We all love Rose and Jack from that movie, classic! Now guess who "The Buyers" are? We are.

Life can get so consuming until we literally sleep through moments when others are trying to take advantage of us. Don't you hate it when you've been seeing someone for a while or even a week and all of sudden you find out they're attached, a terrorist, engaged or married, not human? Or when you go buy a product or subscribe to a service and it's not even close to what they said it would be? These are prime cases of The Liars & The Buyers. It's the way of the world but you can put a stop to it today, at least in your personal life. I suggest you ask every question known to man when you meet someone. Some dating experts say certain questions are off limits when you first meet someone, I totally disagree. Wasting my time is off limits, can I get an Amen? The voices in my head just said "Amen" so you don't have to respond. Maybe some sexual questions can be put off until later but everything else should be pretty much an open book. Who wants to wait six months to a year, then end up separating because you didn't know she was born a man or that he fantasizes about eating angels or children. Trust me, this kind of stuff really happens.

I'm not letting the corporations off that easily, some are just as bad. They'll do and say whatever they have to, to make money. People will do and say whatever they have to as well to get into your world and your bank account. Not to be paranoid about it, but the smile across the room is only the start. Give them the benefit of the doubt, but stay alert, you never know what The Liars are capable of these days. Just stay off the menu. Bon Appetite!

DAY 4
GO FOR A WALK.

I'm a true advocate for solitude and I believe there's nothing greater or more valuable than spending time with yourself to reflect, refresh your mind, take it easy and breathe fresh air. I find that the best way to accomplish this is by taking a walk, preferably somewhere peaceful where there's not a lot going on to distract you from nature and yourself. You can take your cell phone but turn it off, you only need to hear from within and not from the ten people texting and calling you back to back. I suggest you walk alone. You can walk with a friend, significant other or family member close behind, as long as they know the purpose of the walk is for solitude. The last thing you need to hear is the latest family, neighborhood or celebrity gossip. It may be hard to find time for the walk but make it happen. Becoming a success and remaining successful can take up great amounts of time and energy, leaving very few moments to check in with yourself. No matter how great your success is, communion with self will always be greater and worth more than any amount of success.

Using this time alone helps you clear your mind so you can listen to your ideas and make greater decisions. It gives you a clean slate to figure out what you want, what you don't want,

what you need to change and who needs the next STOP sign. Too much business-oriented things in your life can be harmful. Too many voices in your life can be detrimental. There has to be a balance somewhere, we only have so many hours in a day. Taking a walk is not only great for your mind and spirit but also for your body and your heart.

Photo courtesy of BostonBiker.org

DAY 5
KNOW YOUR TYPE.

I believe that being successful is a choice just as much as I believe that being a failure and accepting defeat is also a choice. We all know what type of clothes we like, the types of food we enjoy eating and the type of movies and television shows we like to watch. If you're going to date or look for someone to date, I think you should at least know what you desire this person to be like. Some people, even relationship experts say that you shouldn't have a list of things you expect when meeting someone new, I totally disagree. Casual dating is for people who have nothing better to do. Meeting someone new week after week, year after year, that's ridiculous and a waste, unless you're getting free meals each time.

I say have a basic list, not long, but a short list of must-haves the other person should bring to the table, this way you can save time on the phone, texting, meeting, water from the shower, electricity, wardrobe, you name it. If you're anything like me, you hate wasting time, especially wasting time on something that isn't going to benefit you in no way, shape, fashion or form in the long run. To bypass the years of wasting time, like millions of people do every annually, my advice is to know your type. Certain things could vary from person to person, and you may give a hottie (a very attractive person) the benefit of the doubt or a pass, but your basics should apply to everyone. Example, if they can read and write, that might be a good quality to look for, I hope so. Some people can date a smoker, some can't. I personally can't do the snoring thing because I'm a lite sleeper but that can be handled medically for most snorers. Other basics could include their spirituality, whether they want/like or don't want/dislike children, their career status, whatever it may be, define your basics as soon as possible. If you're still single in two or three years, then maybe you need to ease up on some of the basics, or it could be that people just aren't measuring up in the area where you live or through the avenues you are using to meet them. It could also be the trending culture. I've discovered that some people are more open to long-term relationships who live in certain regions and countries, while in others, being "friends with benefits" is the new marriage.

DAY 6
DON'T BE TOO AVAILABLE.

The last thing you need is to be known around town as the person who was on a date with this person one night, another person the next night, then someone else that weekend. It's time consuming and way too risky for your reputation, especially if you aren't making any progress. I remember hanging out with this one female, we were just friends, seriously, just friends, but people assumed other things as they do, and began to tell me all about her past rendezvous and her history of sorts. I never asked her about it or cared, I just enjoyed hanging out with her, but because she was available to so many others in the past, word traveled to me instantly, almost like a warning sign. Everywhere we went people would look at me strangely, I had no clue she was that popular or known, and not in a good way. The moral of the story is, be more exclusive if you decide to date, don't meet just anyone or everybody, anytime and anywhere. There is an expanding circle of serial daters out there, the regulars who will never settle down but are just waiting to include your name in the pool for conversation or even judgment.

Success can breeds envy, flattery, plenty of admiration and several more things, some that are welcomed, others that are shunned. From my experiences, people tend to gravitate more to the successful, wanting and requesting more of their time, desiring to affiliate with them and what they represent in order to enhance their own life or image, and doing whatever they have to, to get their attention. Opportunities become more frequent and sooner or later someone will stamp you as an "expert" in your field. It can all get overwhelming if not careful. Being too available to everyone will often result in overexposure and eventually burn out. I've experienced this firsthand. Balance must take center stage and discipline has to direct the show. You can't stop people from wanting to communicate with you and requesting your attendance or opinion, but you can learn the importance and the power of saying "No". Though I hate turning down opportunities, some just aren't worth my health and peace of mind. Several aren't even a part of my vision and life mission. Be wise to filter through the all hoopla that success can bring. If not wise, the mishandling of your greatest success can be the greatest threat to failure.

Running around town or around the world for that matter is tiring. Being single actually has its benefits but who really wants to remain single? I don't think anyone does. I believe there are moments in our lives, especially as a single business professional, where being single is a must, depending on how many coals you have in the fire professionally, it can be hard to juggle a relationship or even find time to talk on the phone with someone outside of business. I guess it's all matter of perspective and knowing what you can and cannot handle, as well as what you want and do not want. Don't lose any sleep over it though, most things happen when they're suppose to. Oddly, it always seems harder to meet someone when you're looking and easier to when you're not. Just sleep on it and don't spread yourself too thin by being available to everyone, all the time. Most of it can wait.

DAY 7
BREAKFAST ANYONE?

The older I get the more I realize just how important morning breakfast is. I've stopped drinking milk because I don't understand it. I can't go near scrambled eggs because I keep thinking about that little baby birdie that was inside the shell, and most sausage is made of so many things until it frustrates me, yet I still have to find something to fulfill, refresh and refuel my body at the start of the day. Whether you are a morning person or not, what you do in the morning can have a lasting effect on you for the rest of the day, hopefully a positive effect. If you're out there in the dating scene, you should try a breakfast date. I can only imagine how different it is from an evening date. After waking up you only have a few minutes if that to even think, unlike waiting all day for an evening outing, then pondering, getting nervous, and canceling at the last minute. People are nicer in the morning or they pretend to be, saying "Good morning" as if they're truly excited to be out of that soft bed, I don't think so people. Maybe the potential of better dates is hidden in the rise and shine hours. Try it, let me know how it goes.

They say breakfast is the most important meal of the day, rightly so, because it strengthens you and helps empower the bloodstream, muscles, organs and vessels to get you on your way. It works the same for business and success. What you do in the morning or when you wake up prepares you for what's ahead. Every highly successful person I know has or has had some type of morning or wake-up routine, whether it's studying, meditation, worship, writing, working out, reading or whatever gets their mind, body and/or spirit alert. When I wake up, I'm often trying to figure what day of the week it is, days don't always feel like the days of the week anymore. Working constantly or too much could cause this, so try not to get to the point where I used to be, and end up missing days of the week. There were mornings (and still to this day) I'd wake up and it's Wednesday, then 24 hours later it's Friday and I'm like where did Thursday go? I hope I'm not the only one who has experienced that. If I am, don't tell anyone.

What's your morning, start-of-the-day, or wake-up routine like? Shower, wash your face, brush your teeth, grab a honey bun and go? Sounds like my routine. We all can do better. Try to incorporate some of the same things that the world's most successful do. If you have to go to bed earlier and get up earlier then do what needs to be done, successful people are familiar with sacrifice. Your success must be for a lifetime and even outlast your lifetime. Some people can't get out of bed in time for breakfast. I recall days when I never ate breakfast, it felt as if I had no appetite, my body had become so accustomed to not receiving food before 12pm until it completely adjusted to that schedule. Though I feel like an idiot saying this now, I recently discovered that my business ideas, alertness and instinct are more frequent, more attuned and more on point when I manage to get some type of breakfast in. If you're used to missing out on your morning nutrition, I suggest a change, immediately, give it a try. It could change your life and your level of success. It definitely worked for me.

DAY 8
SINGLE BY CHOICE OR SINGLE BY NECESSITY

Being single is not a bad thing unless not being single is your hearts' desire. It used to be that people would say they're single because they can't find anyone suitable to be with. Nowadays, there's a new culture who claim they are single by choice and actually like it. Some of this new breed believes that heartache is inevitable and that everyone they meet tends to be either untrustworthy or just a waste of time. I completely understand where they are coming from. Still others say they enjoy their freedom and not having to check-in with someone else or be accountable for their actions. We all know where that is going. So if you know someone who claims to be *Single By Choice* yet they complain a lot about being single, just pull out your STOP sign or remind them of their decision, after all, they are single by choice.

    We've entered a new era of entrepreneurs and business professionals where there are more single individuals branching out into owning their own business and pursuing their dreams, many of whom have put their personal life on the back burner in order to focus entirely on their career goals. These individuals declare that they are *Single By Necessity*. I can't argue at all with this because I believe at this point in my life, I just may fall in that same category as well. After a few failed relationships or two, if you've observed patterns, how things work, the amount of time needed to nurture and grow the relationship, you should have more than enough knowledge to apply toward future relationships, plus be able to decipher rather or not the timing is right for a new one. Some can juggle a relationship with their work, others can't. Having self-imposed or work imposed deadlines can consume much of your emotional and mental capacity, causing one to be *Single By Necessity*. I don't think it's a bad thing as long as you're able to balance it all. True enough, when you're determined to be beyond successful, the only concern you have is achieving success. It's a choice that we all have to make and for some it's more of a mandate, so don't judge people if they pursue success over love for the time being or forever, it's their thing.

Is it just me or does it ever feel to you like the hours of the day are getting shorter and shorter? I often wish there were thirty-six hours in a day and at least eight days in a week. Do you ever feel like you need more time and more days? I'm like, where I am suppose to schedule sleep in? I know, life is a balancing act. Technology continues to create more ways for us to waste time as well as save time, it's pretty much a *Catch 22* no matter how you look at it. It will take great discipline and even disappointing people to really get yourself on track to where you have time for others, yourself and a possible mate. Just make sure you're getting enough rest more than anything else or you'll be cranky and moody. When that happens, you won't be *Single By Choice*, nor will you be *Single By Necessity*, you'll be *Single By Attitude,* and I'm sure you know a few those people already.

DAY 9
THE POWER OF SLEEP.

This book wouldn't be complete without addressing "sleep". Though I feel like I need very little sleep, it doesn't mean that it's right. It's actually bad, especially if you're single. Now that I think of it, lack of sleep could be the reason why some single people are single. Nothing within the human body truly operates at its full potential when we're tired and droopy. You sure can't see through someone who pretends to be interested in you if you can hardly keep your eyes open physically. We even age faster from lack of sleep. I'm sure some of you want to close this book right now and take a nap because of that statement, but yes friends, though the word "Sleepy" lends to humor in the book title, and that was clearly my intention, still, it's not a laughing matter when it comes to making daily life decisions. Rest is more important than we know but as time has progressed, it appears to be becoming more difficult to schedule rest with all of our responsibilities, gadgets and distractions. One moment, I have a text to respond to, be right back.

Ok I'm back. Life itself is distracting. The more people you have in your life, the less sleep you will get, unless they are encouraging you to get more rest. Add in success without some type of discipline or power nap schedule, and you'll be in the hospital before you know it. You'll be 28 years old yet looking like 78, or 50 feeling 105, been there, done that. When it comes to success, you may develop a love and hate relationship with sleep. There are days I wish we didn't need it. It can be such a waste of time, just like other mandatory things the human body has to do. Honestly, I experience moments where I'm like, can't I just push a button and have this done already? Our body is fragile, extremely fragile, even though it can self-heal, it cannot re-energize itself without our help, so we'll need to pitch in at some point, especially when you have major deadlines, launches, appearances and business-oriented responsibilities to tend to. It's even hard to negotiate and sift opportunities when you're restless. I've canceled plenty of meetings in the past when I knew my mental and physical fuel was on empty. I'm glad I did though. We can't cancel all meetings so in this case we have no choice but to play by the human body rules, rest is inevitable. That's one thing that we can't control, unfortunately.

I don't like feeling sleepy. Most successful people that I know are still learning to balance work and sleep, it can take a while, even a lifetime. You know, I'm not sure if I even like to sleep. I get offended by people who sleep too much, strangely, especially when I know they have gifts and talents that need to be realized, released and acted upon. I'd rather be up accomplishing something, creating something or eating. Sleep is so boring. I feel great when I wake up rested so maybe I'll keep it as a part of my daily routine, and this eight hours of sleep thing that we're suppose to get? Sounds almost impossible right? Rest more if you can, it really will make a huge difference in everything you do and pursue, as well as those who pursue you.

DAY 10
DINNER ON ME.

There's power in taking the first step and making the first move. That doesn't mean email me and ask me to marry you, just had to add that in. Most of my life I've lived the complete opposite, believe it or not. In my earlier days, I was always the one waiting around from someone to approach me, praying for an opportunity to come in the mailbox or to my front door. Thinking that way didn't get me very far, not even pass the front door. After observing people, their mindsets, emotions and responses, I discovered that the person who normally offers, proposes or presents something, no matter what it is, has a better chance for success in getting exactly what they want. Why is this? People like being catered to, people want to feel special, wanted, desired, included and appreciated.

Nothing makes someone feel more appreciated and valued than you offering to take them to lunch, dinner, a movie, or including them in a philanthropic project or business venture.

You'll never meet that special someone if your approach is always to wait on them to appear. Most things in life you'll have to approach yourself, at least meet them half way. You should remain open to new things, meeting new people, new opportunities, new ideas and allow the unlimited atmosphere that is available everyday to meet you face to face. Millions live life going through the same schedule and daily routines. You have to make a conscious internal decision to welcome the unexpected while also expecting greater things to appear and happen. Living with a desire to be more, see more and have more appear in your life.

You'd be amazed how many Yes's you can get, how many open doors and contacts you can bring into your life just by taking the initiative and making the first move. Of course there's the risk of rejection and the big NO, but risk is our middle name So go ahead and invite someone on a date, they're probably waiting on you to ask. I can't wait to see how many invites I get from that sentence. Contact a nonprofit organization and volunteer, I'm sure many of them are praying for your call. And just think of the millions of business professionals seeking to be a part of something or better yet, have you take interest in what they're doing. Make the call, send the email, text your existence away, get involved, open up your life to more. Self-starters run the world while the world watches. Those who wait too long normally get ignored and end up receiving the leftovers if any are available. Timing is crucial. The majority of the world follows the lead of the bold and the successful, which means as you become bolder and more successful, there are millions if not billions of people waiting to support you and ready to give you what you want.

Q&A WITH
TORRY WILLIAMS
OWNER, ICONS BAR & GRILL

1. What was your most awkward or worst dating experience?

Answer: I hate to say it but I stopped-up the toilet during a date.

2. Have you ever been misled by someone who was interested in you? If so, what was the experience like?

Answer: Yes, a female got my number from a cousin of mine. When I spoke with this female on the phone, she described herself as 'model material' but when we met in person, I believe she left the 'model' at home.

3. **What was the worst or most hilarious lie you've ever been told by someone you were dating or intending to date?**

Answer: My ex-girlfriend told me she was straight as in heterosexual but I found out later that this wasn't true.

4. **If your friends had to describe your dating life in one word, what would that word be?**

Answer: Pimped-Out.

5. **In your opinion, has social media sites complicated the dating world, helped it or a little bit of both?**

Answer: I believe it's equally beneficial and equally destructive but it's all a matter of how you use it and the moral compass of the person.

6. **Have you ever went to see a movie alone?**

Answer: Yes

7. **Is seven days a week enough days for you or do you need more days, if so how many?**

Answer: Not sure if I need more or less. The more days the more bills, I just need to make more money.

8. **If you had more time what would you do with it, how would you use it?**

Answer: I'd use it to nurture my relationships more with my family, nieces and nephews.

9a. **How many hours of sleep do you get in a night?**

Answer: Five

9b. **How many hours of sleep would you like to get?**

Answer: Eight

10. **How do you feel about texting?**

Answer: I only text when I need to. I'd rather talk on the phone.

11. **If you were given an extra million dollars today, what is the first thing you'd buy with it or use it for?**

Answer: I'd pay off all of my mom's bills.

12. **What do you think are some of the key ingredients to a successful relationship or marriage?**

Answer: Chemistry, compatibility, things in common. Patience. Forgiveness. Both individuals being nonjudgmental towards one another.

13. **What do you think are some of the key ingredients to being successful in life and in**

business?

Answer: Being like a thermostat, not a thermometer, so you can set the tone and the temperature. Learning how to be aggressive and take control. Never limiting yourself or confining yourself to one way of thinking or one way of doing things. Building your professional network of contacts. Prayer.

DAY 11
THE NEW NORMAL.

Is being single the new married? It feels like it. I mean, every other day there's news of another marriage split (mostly in Hollywood), another couple breaking up or someone being caught cheating (mostly in the neighborhood). Single retreats, singe night-outs, singles networking, single's book clubs, single's restaurants, single's bowling alleys, the list has grown to where it makes you wonder if single really is the new normal. I'm not sure if it's the fact that people have more options now to meet other people and mingle (you can thank or frown upon social media for that) or if it's a question of whether people still have the patience to get to know someone. The norm has become the abnormal, and now the abnormal is the new norm. Don't get me wrong, not everyone falls into the new normal category or mindset.

It's safe to say that the norm to becoming successful is also out the door as well. At one point we were all told to go to school, graduate from college, do this, do that and we'll be successful. Well, that's the furthest thing from the truth from what I've learned. Though it's smart and a must to be educated, I can't honestly say that it's a guaranteed way to success. There are hundreds of very educated, multiple degree professionals and individuals sending me their resumes for employment, when I've never even touched a college degree in my life. Talent and instinct alone can make you successful whether you know how to read or write, sadly. I prefer to have the talent, skill, plus be able to read and write though. Having a great idea mixed with the passion and skill set to produce that idea into reality, can also make you successful. Don't get me wrong, hard work will always be a necessity if you want any meaningful success but there's no definite path to follow anymore. The unbelievable amount of successful entrepreneurs springing up around the world today can attest to that. Social media has opened up the entire planet to us and the limits have been removed.

During our earlier era of human existence, daylight meant wake up, work the land. Nightfall meant go to sleep and no man should work, but our present new normal is work until you're rich, sleep when you're dead. A new normal isn't necessarily a bad thing, some are, but not all. As long as we maintain respect for one another and continue to learn from our past and present mistakes, we'll be just fine. Think on this, what are your new normals?

DAY 12
THE POWER OF COMMITMENT.

Oh no, it's time for the undeniable "C" word, yes, the word that separates the men from the boys, women from the girls, relationships from one night relations, entrepreneurs from the wantrepreneurs, the Fortune 500's from the start-ups that lose momentum after three months. Welcome to the world of commitment. Options are many, which means commitment to anything or anyone is pretty much, optional. Sad but true, several singles remain single because of commitment issues, within themselves or by noticing the issues within the other person. We get hurt in unhealthy relationships, letting those memories carry over, willing and ready to sabotage any future hope of happiness with someone new. When emotions start knocking we pull away, run away for some. I've been there, feeling awkward in that moment, especially when all you hear around you is negativity and news of breakups and so on. It's easier said than done to think positive in the midst of a world that constantly appears to have gone madd, but in order to maintain sanity and at least have the chance of happiness, we have to stow our fears, pride and phobias, depart into the possibilities and arrive into what could be. Lots of airplane terminology there, due to too many flights I tell you. But that's it, we're risk takers and this is what we must do in order to find happiness in anything.

Every business professional must come face to face with commitment. Most business owners have a plan, yet when that plan isn't going like they expected, a decision must be made. Whether to continue and remain committed will always come into question. It's a characteristic of maturity and growth, a sister to discipline, and a prerequisite to becoming great. There is no Greatness without commitment, no Success without discipline and no Guidance without maturity. No matter which way you look at it, commitment can be frightening, uncertain and risky. You're sacrificing time, energy and most likely money as well. One thing I do know, you'll never know what could have been, how far you could have gone, how much happiness you could have experienced, how long it could have lasted and how many people you could have helped, if you don't commit to something.

DAY 13
LISTEN TO YOUR PEACE.

Over the years I've learned that apart from using knowledge, research, facts and proper information to make a sound and great decision, it is my level of peace that ultimately makes me comfortable when making that decision. What do I mean by peace? Simply put, feeling that everything is OK and not being tensed, nervous or experiencing any anxiety about the matter. You know how you meet someone new for the first time, take for example a first date. After talking to that person, checking out their responses, their roaming eyes, their gestures and so on, something within you may tell you that this date needs to end early. You have no peace about continuing the date or seeing that person again, ever. Several people go through life not trusting their instinct, which is usually in conjunction with your peace. Listen to your peace to avoid making bad decisions.

Our inner peace always alerts us when something doesn't feel right, also when something does. It's either a level of frustration, doubt and concern that won't go away or it's a surge of confidence and assurance that makes you want to shout for joy. Your awareness of the level of peace you have in circumstances concerning every area of your life should be added to other information you've obtained before you make any decisions. It could be as small as what to wear to an event. Listen to your peace, deciding on what makes you feel most comfortable and represents you best in that setting.

By following and listening to my peace, I feel more confident and more powerful in every aspect of my life. More confident in what I do, what I refuse to do, who I see and who I'd rather not see. More powerful in my business decisions and long-term decisions for myself and for others. Learning to listen to your peace can save you a lot of heartache, mistakes and several wasted years of your life.

DAY 14
TO TEXT OR NOT TO TEXT.

Do people talk on the phone anymore? Does anyone know their actual phone number? Where did the home land lines go? Well friends, as we all know, unless you're living under a FlintStone rock, text messages have taken over, seriously. You can even text globally for free now, anywhere on the planet. Kids are texting, teachers are texting, cats and dogs are texting, world leaders are even texting each other. Is this benefiting us or destroying human communication and relationships? We've entered into a new era that's for sure, one that hasn't been proven to be all good or all bad as of yet, but if you're single and considering dating, you should establish when it's best to text and when it's not. There are things that can't be expressed properly through words on a screen alone, and more than enough arguments and breakups have occurred due to texts that were misunderstood. Texting has several benefits, it's easy, instant and you can reach a boat load of people at the same time without calling them all separately one by one. Isn't that what we all desire though, to be able to say "Good morning, have a great day" to 1,000 friends with the push of a button?

More than not have I used texting, especially in business. Information is rampant, there's no other way to keep up with everyone and everything as fast, other than by text. Instant notifications can not only save your business and your job, they can save your life. Nothing will ever replace that business call or the lunch or dinner meeting face to face, human to human interaction will always be around, no matter how advanced we get. As long as trusting someone is a requirement, in-person interaction will remain. Relationships benefit by instant messages by saying things like "Just thinking about you". Those tidbits can be immediately comforting to someone who can't receive a call from you at that time.

Texting has also ushered in a very short way

to even make life-changing decisions electronically so you don't have to deal physically with someone if they were in your actual presence. Texts such as "You're fired", "I want a divorce", "I'm cheating on you", and more have become ever so popular in the past few years. It's all a matter of usage though. When was the last time you actually talked to the person you're interested in dating or meeting, or has it only been texting, for three months now? We must be careful of any new technology while still using it to benefit our own lives. Computers are created by man, without us they wouldn't exist. They'll never replace the human race, not entirely. The same for texting, it'll never replace the soul soothing and comfort of hearing an actual voice nor will it ever replace the excitement or assurance of meeting someone in person. By the way, I recently had to hire a texter, that is, someone to text and respond to people for me. Saves me hours and hours of time so I can focus on other things, like meet more people in person that my texter can text for me. Come on, I'm just joking. Believe it or not, people are now sharing how many TPM's they can do on their resumes, Texts Per Minute. The times have truly changed.

DAY 15
THE AWKWARD.
THE UNEXPECTED.
THE UNPREDICTABLE.

I believe being a single professional opens your life up to more awkward moments than the average person, especially when others know that you're single. There's nothing more awkward than a friend hooking you up on a date with someone you have remotely no interest in. You can expect just about anyone to approach you when people know you're single, and if they know you're successful on top of that, beware. I've experienced it all, from people hitting on me in the airport, at restaurants, at road STOP signs, in the library, at the post office, in the grocery store, at the hotel ice machine, and yes, in the bathroom. Sometimes I think it's better to wear an engagement ring so I'm not approached or stared at or winked at or followed, it really happens. Maybe your life isn't as dramatic but never say never.

One thing we can't change is the unexpected, so don't get upset, scared or mad when you're approached by someone who should already know not to approach you, and we all know those types. Take it as a compliment, that's what I do, well I try to. Now if they start sending you gifts, somehow get your number without you giving it to them or following you around Walmart, then you may need to take greater precaution. The more successful you are, the more unpredictable onlookers can become. Of course things are easier if you live a bit of a sheltered life but we all aren't able to have security 24/7 unfortunately or work from home. If you can, then great, if not, you'll need to be more aware of your surroundings, not just in public, but on the computer as well, and that cell phone, it's becoming a world of its own to look out for.

DAY 16
ROAD TRIP OF A LIFETIME.

I've made it mandatory to seek out people to teach me from their mistakes. This may sound cruel or even funny, but to me it's genius. You could spend your entire life wanting to learn and figure things out for yourself, make your own mistakes, learn the hard way, and all that nonsense or you can connect with those who have already traveled down those roads, who are willing to be your guide and give you directions. Whether it's friends, parents, teachers, other family members or even strangers, just about everyone you meet or know has more experience in something than you do. This is a great thing, now all you need to do is ask questions. A lot of today's single professionals think we know it all, we're hot, sexy, successful, can have anyone and anything we want (as some think), and believe that we can Google just about any concern we have, when googling is still getting the opinion of someone else. Just how authentic and factual are answers on the internet anyway? Be cautious with that. It's better to get your information from those who can tell you like it is, from a real human to human experienced-based viewpoint. Don't spend the rest of your life, spending the rest of your life, trying to figure out something that can take less than a minute to settle.

Any business professional who doesn't research their career or industry ahead of time is an unwise individual. There are those who are doing what you desire, those who have mastered what it is you want to become. These are the people that can save you time, money and heartache if you just ask for advice, consultation or to be mentored. I'm constantly sharing my business, publishing, event services and entertainment industry experience with thousands of people around the world. Use others for your road signs, find those who have traveled to those destinations, find several. Learn about the trips from them, so that your pursuits are more rewarding and fulfilling. You'll also have less bumps, can avoid road blocks and the endless road reconstruction zones that continue throughout life.

DAY 17
SOLITUDE VS. LONELINESS.

Of course you can be in a relationship and still experience loneliness. Not every relationship is fulfilling but if you are in one or decide to be in one, it's probably not the right one if you still feel lonely. Something's not right with that picture. There are times when we'd rather be single and be alone until we feel we are ready to be in a relationship or in another relationship, but I don't believe it's the desire of anyone's heart to endure loneliness. We weren't created to be alone or to experience life alone. People were created for one another, so don't let any fears, lack of knowledge, lack of technology, lack of social skills or anything of the such keep you from meeting new people. Our lives should expand in some way with every new person we meet. It's important that we are always observant of this.

Then there's solitude. This is an intentional place that you put yourself in. It actually has nothing to do with being single or in a relationship. Solitude isn't talked about enough, nor do people realize how important it is. Oftentimes we need to step back to listen from within, analyze things or emotions going on in our lives, so we can make greater decisions. Solitude isn't a time of loneliness, it's a time of learning. Even if you're in a relationship, you need solitude every now and then to make yourself better for that relationship. The world itself would be better if we all stopped for a while to think before we do or say things. Ponder on that. One moment of thinking could prevent a lifetime of suffering.

Embrace solitude while at the same time opening your life to others that you trust. Don't let loneliness win the battle. You're amazing, a unique creation, and there's a group of people that were created to be a part of your life, you just have to find them. And if you desire that special someone, they're out there too. It's a matter of believing and pursuing. That's life, believing and pursuing, the path to fulfillment and happiness in a nutshell.

DAY 18
CHILDREN OR NO CHILDREN?

"**S**ingle" and "Successful", just decades ago it would have been hard to figure out where to add in kids with those two words but the world has truly changed, and there could possibly more single and successful parents than there are married ones, if not, then I'm sure they are gaining ground. Whether you decide to marry, remain single, become a monk as my good friend fashion designer Curry Armand claims he will become sooner or later, or whatever the case, making the decision to bring a child or children into your life is one that we all must face at some point. For many it's easy and obvious, for others it's a tough life decision, especially if career is the primary focus. The older we get, the future should remain on our minds. If you haven't decided on children yet, I suggest setting an age to where you have to make that decision, whether to have your own or adopt. Don't get mad but I'd be really happy to have a son if he comes out of the womb already at twelve years old. That way we can get straight to work on running these businesses and writing more books. I know, I sound like a totally impatient time-managing lunatic. OK sorry, he can come out at four years old, already talking and walking because we have places to go and people to meet.

Just like being in a relationship takes commitment, so does having children, a life commitment. You can't divorce them though some parents try, and don't kick them to the curb for being unfaithful. We can't only be the best in our careers, we must strive to be the best parents we can possibly be as well. We're responsible to guide and mentor these new young minds just like we've guided our successes. From what I hear, what I've seen and what I've learned, here is where the word "Sleepy" comes into play as far as the book title. They say that children can cause you to lose far more sleep than your career over a lifetime, so be ready for a few sleepless nights, maybe weeks, month, possibly years, hopefully too many though.

DAY 19
NOTHING ON TV. CREATE YOUR OWN SHOW.

Now don't get the wrong idea about the topic title, we've witnessed more than enough videos going viral around the world from the privacy of a home, so I'm not talking about one of those shows. Can someone be successful and bored with the success? You'd be surprised how many successful singles fall into this category. Having everything you need while not having what you really want. It's impossible to learn it all, see it all and experience it all in one lifetime, so there's always something more to do, learn, explore, create or even innovate. Being single frees up time to do things that you've always dreamed of doing. Not everyone was meant to be coupled believe it not. Single with a pet is the new married. Companionship and friendship with other human beings is mandatory for growth but an actual love and intimate relationship with another is not. So if there's nothing going on in that area of your life, create something else to replace it. Use that energy or that time to enhance your life in some way or work toward enhancing another person's life.

Some of the most influential and legendary people in history were single. Nikola Tesla said love was a distraction to his focus and he was by far one of the most amazing inventors and people to ever walk the planet. The famous peanut revolutionary George Washington Carver rocked the same boat, remaining single throughout life though he did try at least one relationship. Whether you agree with Tesla or Carver's singleness or not, it's still up to you to fill those spaces in your life and continue to move forward. Mentoring and volunteering may be something you should look into, just don't encourage the viral video movement. There are millions of young people and adults that can use what you know, your expertise, your advice, your friendship. There's nothing wrong with being single and there's nothing wrong with being in a relationship, but there is something wrong with wasting your life away in either situation and not using it to its full potential. Stay in a constant state of progression and you'll attract everything in your life that was meant to meet you.

DAY 20
THE PICKUP LINE VS. THE ELEVATOR PITCH.

You never know when you'll be in a position or situation to market yourself, a business idea or even to meet a potential life partner. It could happen any day, almost anywhere, at any moment. Will you be ready if and when it presents itself? Do you have a tested pickup line prepared? What about your response to a pickup line? Heard any good elevator pitches lately? The most important thing to remember is your presentation, meaning how you want to appear to the other person or group of people. You need to be clear about what you want and don't want, so those listening will not get the wrong idea. It happens all the time. Doesn't matter if you're in a bar or a business meeting, clarity is what you need to give people from the start, this saves a lot of time and confusion.

Though the pickup line is normally used in the dating world and the elevator pitch in business, they can sometimes cross pollinate, especially in today's society where business and pleasure has created its own industry. Both are planned out, scripted and rehearsed 99% of the time, both should be short yet to the point and either could change your life. The tables do turn however and you may be the one rehearsing a pickup line or elevator pitch, so learn from the ones that others approach you with or even those you noticed being used on others. If that doesn't work, get ideas from Hollywood movies, they are laced with them. Give advice to those who deliver stale elevator pitches and by all means give advice to anyone who comes at you with a ridiculous pickup line that a money-hungry cab driver wouldn't even pick up.

Q&A WITH
ADRIENNE NOEL
CEO, MARKETING MINDS AT WORK

1. What was your most awkward or worst dating experience?

Answer: From time to time I do online dating. A guy approached me, he had a very interesting profile, lots of photos. We had amazing phone conversations over time. One day I invited him out to a local event, he declined. The next week I invited him to another event, he declined a second time. Days later he offered to meet at the local mall. When I met him, it was obvious the photos he used online were at least 15 to 20 years old. You can pretty much figure out the rest of that story.

2. **If your friends had to describe your dating life in one word, what would that word be?**

Answer: Roller-coaster.

3. **In your opinion, has social media sites complicated the dating world, helped it or a little bit of both?**

Answer: A bit of both but I believe the best time and the best way to meet someone is when you're in college, people are much easier to meet. You're constantly surrounded by several individuals daily and for the most part, you have to interact with them on some level. As you get older and each year passes by, I believe that it becomes more difficult to meet people because most are already focused on their individual track.

4. **Have you ever went to see a movie alone?**

Answer: Yes.

5. Are you still friends with past lovers or was the entire relationship ruined?

Answer: In most cases I am friends with them. I find that it's important but sometimes it can be very difficult.

6. Is seven days a week enough days for you or do you need more days, if so how many?

Answer: Seven is fine.

7. Is twenty-four hours a day enough hours for you, or do you need more hours, if so, how many?

Answer: Two or three more hours would be great.

8. If you had more time what would you do with it, how would you use it?

Answer: I'd spend more time with my daughter and I'd get out more to try and meet someone special.

9. How many hours of sleep do you get in a night?

Answer: About four hours.

10. How many hours of sleep would you like to get?

Answer: Eight

11. How do you feel about texting?

Answer: I don't like texting.

12. If you were given an extra million dollars today, what is the first thing you'd buy with it or use it for?

Answer: First thing, I'd pay off mortgage, then put aside college tuition for my daughter and go on a trip around the world. I'd definitely go back to Brazil, I love it there.

13. What do you think are some of the key ingredients to a successful relationship or marriage?

Answer: Communication is the first, closely followed by Respect.

14. What do you think are some of the key ingredients to being successful in life and in business?

Answer: Communication and respect as well. Having open communication at all times to explain to the other party how I feel, what I want and desire, and they do the same.

15. Are you Single By Choice or Single By Necessity?

Answer: I'm single and looking.

DAY 21
SOCIAL MEDIA DO'S AND DON'TS.

If you're single and not a part of the online social media generation in some facet, then you may not be alive, yet I completely understand your decision. In the meantime, check your pulse. Facebook, Instagram, Twitter, Linkedin, the seven million dating sites, you name it, they're all available and continue to grow every single day. Social media comes with great benefits for the single professional and the disadvantages follow closely behind. So what are we to make of this new machine that connects you with almost anyone in the world, instantly? Well, any smart business professional, networker, visionary or entrepreneur would tell you to use it to your advantage. If it's chatting and reconnecting with old friends, looking for a life partner or business networking, it would only make sense to take advantage of it but keep in mind that your privacy may not be altogether private. Knowing this, there are few things I would do and not do, introducing my "Social Media Do's and Don'ts". You may agree or disagree with me on them but that's absolutely fine.

MY SOCIAL MEDIA DO'S AND DON'TS

DON'T: For the more "public" social networks, the big boys, those that everyone have access to, I honestly don't understand why some people place their personal phone numbers on their profile. Yes, I can understand if you're running a business and using it as your business number but if not, this is a total social media Don't.

DON'T: If you're going to include your birthday, don't include the year, that's another don't.

DO: You can include your birthday month and the day for now only, that's a Do.

DON'T: Never put your home address on any

social network, still can't believe some people are actually doing that, definite Don't. I can't believe I'd even have to put this on the list.

DON'T: Don't be so quick to add others to your friends list, network or contacts. Not everyone has your best interest in mind, another Don't.

DO: Instead, check to see who they know, if you have any mutual connections or even ask another person if they know that individual. The more background information you have, the better.

Though these may sound pretty basic, this is all the information hackers and identity thieves need to start interrupting the lives of millions around the world. A lot of people think that hackers need your Social Security Number to steal your identity, not anymore and if they do need it, they can get that elsewhere. With the strategic teams of criminals, frauds and cons working in just about every business industry and government sector, it's becoming much easier now for them to obtain this information. I've heard some crazy stories and I too was once a victim of identity theft. One single professional I know discovered that she'd gotten married a year prior and received a bank loan for a new house but for some reason, she never knew about either. Looks like someone started a brand new life in her name and planned to live happily-ever-after. Come to find out, she had her phone number, home address and full birthday on one of her social media network profiles for all to see. Luckily the culprits were caught. Maybe you too have heard of a few stories about stalkers and people hacking into social media accounts, sharing personal information with the public, it's pure insanity. The online dating sites are no safer, don't be fooled. Indeed several now claim to screen all members for security but there is no guaranteed security other than you not placing all of your personal business out there for the entire world to see. Make great decisions when it comes to social media in all forms. Have fun but never take your guard down.

DAY 22
DEALING WITH A BROKEN HEART.

We all experience them. We all feel the pain and ache of a broken heart at some point in our lives. We can prevent some but for most we can't. So that we don't get bitter, we can only do our best to perceive and accept them as a part of our growth. Broken hearts arrive in many forms, from being betrayed by a friend, falling out with a family member, a failed business venture, long-term business relationship going sour, a marriage or relationship ending, the list goes on. Being single doesn't exclude you, broken hearts can come out of anywhere at anytime, as they often do. One thing that helps me during those moments and sad seasons is knowing that it's not about who caused the pain. We often point the finger at someone or a variety of people then hold them completely responsible and accountable forever. This is the worst way to live and the wrong way to handle a broken heart.

Though you can't forget the pain, you can still forgive the person and try to understand that we are all human, created with many faults and imperfections. Everyone is capable of causing another pain, consciously and unconsciously. Whether it's love, friendship, family, business, it happens and it's a part of life. We can't control everything, though as business professionals, a lot of us desire to. Learning to let go of the things I couldn't control gave me unbelievable freedom and immeasurable peace. The worry and frustration we carry around daily only harms us. From this day forward, make it mandatory to learn to accept the things you can't change, and I'm not saying let people walk all over you, but for the times when a situation is out of your hands and power to orchestrate, just accept it as a part of your journey. Some of the worst things that happen to you in life may turn out to be your biggest breakthroughs and often supernatural advancements in disguise.

DAY 23
UNANNOUNCED ENVY.

You'll rarely hear a conversation in large affluent social circles about the downside of success, achieving your goals or becoming who you've always wanted to be. It's normally reserved for more private conversations with a small group of individuals, a select few or more often a one on one type mentoring session. Well the downside does exist and if you aren't properly prepared for it, it can destroy everything you've worked so hard to achieve. One thing you must come to realize is that not everyone will be happy for your happiness, whether it involves your personal love life, your career, your purpose or even you just having a great day. There are those who wake up with a mission to spill coffee on you or to give you an unfair parking ticket. I believe this is because the average person is unhappy and unfulfilled within themselves. Your progress and productivity can lead to multiple streams of envy and jealously from others, even those closest to you, as close as the person beside you in bed.

Knowing who you are, what you want, what you desire to accomplish, why you wake up in the morning, completely separates you from I'll say about 75% of the world, possibly more. Huge percentage right? It's true. If you watch the news and study the statistics, it appears that most people are unhappy with their jobs and merely content with their lives. Believe it or not that 75% includes some of your friends, family members, co-workers, church members, business colleagues, even past or current lovers. My solution is to be observant, plus aware of changes and the responses of other people when you announce certain successes, advancements or accomplishments. There is a pattern that envy takes and if you catch it soon enough, you can prevent someone from secretly trying to destroy you behind your back.

I'm not saying everyone is out to get you but if you've encountered true success or made strides in areas of your life that those around you haven't, trust me, someone isn't that happy about it. You can send them all the yellow smiley faces via text and it won't change much. Hopefully they'll get over it, most do when you reach out to them and try to help them find themselves or help them achieve their own dreams and goals. For those who can't seem to shake it, they'll need to be removed, no matter who they are, or you may end up being betrayed down the line. Envy and jealously are very serious emotions, so they have to be dealt with seriously. Never take either lightly, they can carry extremely heavy outcomes and results, even fatal.

DAY 24
MOVIE ANYONE?

Who doesn't love a great movie? We have so many choices throughout the year, all the while hoping that each season presents something different, when of course, the same movie plots often repeat themselves. Some are good, ridiculous, great, frightening, hilarious and plenty waste your time and money. Oh don't forget the Summer blockbusters that everyone waits for and dreams about. So why not go see a movie with a friend or even alone? In a way we can relate the movie process to being in a relationship, though I'm sure we'd all prefer it if Hollywood gave us more of a variety annually.

The single life is like a blank movie ticket. First you need to decide what type of movie you're in the mood for or exactly what do you want to see. Do you want something that's fun, something romantic and intense, something adventurous where you dive in for the challenge, something dramatic, or are you the type that needs a little fatal attraction? Then you decide when you'd like to attend the showing, as in when you're ready to actually put yourself out there to start meeting people. Some of us just wait it out until the Summer, since the best of the best are expected to come out. Whatever the case, you need to know when you want to put the ticket to use. After arriving, you have even more choices to make, very expensive and risky ones, like food and drink. Similar to deciding on the type of person you want to date, you'll need to figure out what are your must-haves and what are your non-negotiables, in other words, things you can't afford to waste time and money on. Hopefully you'll enjoy everything about your choice. Don't overspend by attending too many movies, there are no refunds, so choose wisely.

The blank movie ticket can also apply to business. You have to know when, what type, what you want and don't want, who deserves to be a part of it with you or who doesn't. It's always great to watch movie trailers though, they give you an idea of what you're getting into before you invest your time, energy and money. The more research you have, the better prepared you are in dating and in business. So watch more trailers in life and you'll have the upper hand in it all.

DAY 25
WILLING TO WAIT.

I haven't met anyone around the world yet who likes to wait. I hate waiting but I'm still waiting to find someone who enjoys it. Being a single professional, you will eventually have to accept the unwanted reality of waiting. If you're in school, the process of obtaining your degree will be a wait. If you're starting a business or desire to, the process of getting it to the place where you want it to be will be another wait. Waiting on a significant other? You get where I'm going here. Some things aren't worth waiting on but if it means a lot to you then you'll be willing to wait on it. There are people who go through life, especially a few neurotic business people, trying to rush this and that but there is one thing you can't rush, and that's preparation. It's idiotic to rush into a relationship, no matter how great the emotions are, however in very few cases, it could actually last.

I've been presented many a business opportunities with time limits and deadlines to make a decision right away on the matter. Most of those I just let go, especially if the other party wants a decision within a few hours or days. Indeed some opportunities require a quick response but most should allow you time to let it soak into your thoughts plus give you time to consult your peace. Millions of people desire to do what they've always dreamed of however, without the necessary skills, education or training, this is the mindset of a failure. For life's greatest accomplishments, you'll have to wait on timing and preparation. For life's biggest questions, you'll have to wait on the answers. You can only master this by accepting patience and finding peace with time. Though time waits for no one, we have to wait on it, and allow time to make us better overall. We need it more than it needs us. There is no waiting without time. There is no excellence, achievement or greatness without waiting.

DAY 26
ONLY SLEEP FOR REST OR DEATH.

If we could all get more sleep, the world would probably be a happier place. The world would also be a less innovative and amazing place. I'm sure there would be a huge shortage of everything because no one would be farming or creating as much. As long as the chocolate companies keep producing, I'll survive. Sleep is a beautiful thing, a mandatory part of life to maintain a healthy lifestyle and to stay alive. On the other hand, too much sleep is a direct enemy to the advancement of your life and to the advancement of humanity. Our lives, our creation, our overall being, is one of great invention. What we are capable of as human beings, what we can do, we can create, what we can decipher, what we can build, should blow your mind daily if you meditate on it. Sleeping more than you need to will only hinder your intended productivity in your lifetime. There's nothing wrong with taking much a needed vacation to rest and unwind, nothing at all, but when it's time to resume work, you must return in full power to completely fulfill your journey of life.

DAY 27
LIVE LIFE OR CHANGE IT.

It took me several years to realize that I have the power to change my life and circumstances. I feel an "Oprah" moment coming on right about now. Many of us often wait on a pie to fall out of the sky, I hope it's apple, some wait to win the lottery, while several wait on a miracle from God. Well friends, I'm here to let you know that the fastest way to get what you want out of life and to become what you desire to be, is accomplished by just doing it. Yes, easy to say but in reality, 99% of the time, that's the only way you'll ever see it realized in your life. So many live vicariously through others, following the lives and careers of other people while scrutinizing or praising everything about them instead of living life for themselves. The world watches and judges the successful, the lens is always on them. This is such a sad case but it is our present reality. Your own life should be your main focus and it should be lived with excitement. If you're not the least bit excited when you start your day, then at this exact moment, you need to start preparing for change.

I'm no psychiatrist, thank God, my brain would never rest, but I do know that the human soul and spirit needs love, joy and hope more than anything else. Living unhappy, sad, depressed, tortured, in turmoil, is not OK. If you want a new job or career, stop talking about it, start pursuing it, and keep pursuing it until you get it. If you never get it then create it. If you need new skills, a degree or connections to make it happen, then get started, go back to school. Tired of being single? Start looking for that special someone, don't wait for them to arrive at your door or mailbox, they're not coming, unless FedEx, UPS and USPS start a new in-house service, which could be pretty innovative if you think about it. Nevertheless, if you're in a current relationship that isn't working, either try to fix it, get counseling or dissolve it. Can't stand working for others? Then sit down somewhere or get mentored from a business owner or entrepreneur about starting your own business. Nothing changes until you change it. If you aren't loving your life then you're not really living, you're just surviving. I'm not promising you endless bliss overnight but once you make up in your mind that you want to love life, be happy and be fulfilled, you'll start making strategic decisions toward what it takes to get there and applying yourself every day until you achieve it. You can do this.

DAY 28
A NEW SEASON.

Your awareness of new seasons in your life opens the door to more abundance and your next level of productivity. Change is exciting. Change is risky and for many change is downright frightening, but it's necessary. Some of you reading this are experiencing a new season in your life right now. You're feeling the push to let some people go while allowing new ones to come in. You've now realized that your peace is more important than the unsure and uncertain relationships and friendships you've let linger for so long. It's a new season. Others are discovering that the career you've been in for years or even the one you just started was really not what your heart wanted to do. You've been introduced to your true passions and you understand that at some point you'll have to change directions. It's a new season. Friend, get a new map and head into the direction your passion and true happiness leads.

When seasons change in my life, they too involve evaluating my inner circle, things I'm pursuing personally and business wise, but also placing my thought and decision making processes back under a microscope. It's always wise to look over what we've done in the past, what worked, what didn't work, how you perceived something, in every aspect of our personal and business life. To learn from a past season produces promises for a greater season. The way we think, perceive and analyze life situations, circumstances, decisions and opportunities must continue to grow, to where we are wise enough to share the best way with others in the future. With each new season of life, we should be able to think and operate on a higher level, a wider playing field. By doing so, you become a greater person, reinventing yourself and repositioning yourself to be of greater help to others.

DAY 29
WORK OUT AND WORK IT.

Exercise the body. Exercise the mind. Exercise your spirit. That's a lot of exercising for one person but these three keep you more fit and attuned to life, yourself, the world and your contribution to humanity more than anything else. Single professionals don't have the current responsibilities of raising a family (that is, excluding single parent homes), so in most cases they can have more time than the average professional that has a spouse and kids. They have more availability to focus inward, to get all the pieces of the puzzle together and to become more aware of themselves and what their life needs to produce.

In addition to our outward business life, we also need to maintain a healthy internal business life, that includes knowing when to shake things off and not to worry. We must learn to respect our ideas, love ourselves regardless of our mishaps, exercise our physical body and make time for spiritual growth. If our bodies crash, so does the continued success for most of us. So now more than ever, especially to the single entrepreneurs, we have to pay closer attention to our bodies whether we want to or not. Rest, good food and exercise refreshes the mind. Ideas flow more freely, strategies come easily, creativity hits several highs during these times. There really isn't any excuse for not being able to take fifteen minutes of your day to stretch and do a few exercises. Some people are afraid to say it but I'm not, the average person is just lazy. If you make time to eat you can make time to exercise. That's the truth. I feel better after a short work out and I don't even like working out, I'm already tired from talking about it. I do it because I know my body will reward me if I do, with more energy, alertness and of course a little more sexiness is always welcomed. You don't need a trainer, you don't even need a gym. And for those of you who claim you need someone to motivate you to exercise, let me know who motivates you to eat today. Your body needs you and you need it, it's a partnership, do you part.

DAY 30
THANK GOD FOR PETS.

Could it be true that "Man's best friend" may very well not be man at all? It's amazing how pets have now become roommates and the best friends to so many people, especially singles. I mean, it's understandable why pets are now the new BFF's (best friend forever), road trip passenger, jogging partner and more. They don't talk too much (or at all) so you don't have to worry about them babbling continuously. How many relationships can boast of that benefit? Some pets won't even acknowledge you unless they need something, that sounds familiar. Others will make it known to every visitor and every audible sound that they are the dominant force in the house. Dogs will either lounge in the car seat completely bored or stick their head out of the window to let onlookers know that they're running the entire relationship, signaling to others not to try and come between the two of you. Where would be without our lovely pets? I believe it's high time for me to get one also, a dog of course. I'm naming him "Mango". Mango Moody, perfect!

For you pets owners and pet lovers, have you ever thought about how your pet can sometimes assume a professional business partnership with you? Some of them share the same characteristics as your professional colleagues believe it or not, in a good way, well. Both cats and dogs are guilty of it. Cats can be like silent competitors, appearing innocent, sometimes invisible and no threat on the outside, while always ready to snatch and scratch somebody's head off if they're disrespected or challenged. Dogs can appear like a bonehead business partner making constant bad decisions, sabotaging business deals, so you spend all day and every day cleaning up their poop (you know what word I really mean). It's funny and remarkable, the roles pets play in the lives of the single person. One thing they do show you, regardless of any circumstance, is unconditional love. They're also always there to listen and for the most part, they won't get mad at you. So hats off to the pets of today, making the single life more tolerable and enjoyable. Do something special for your pet this week. They've come to expect the royal treatment since they don't have to share you.

Q&A WITH
STANLEY NWOBI
ACTOR/MARKETER

1. Have you ever been caught off guard by someone flirting with you?

Answer: Yes, it was at work. Very surprised.

2. What was the worst or most hilarious lie you've ever been told by someone you were dating or intending to date?

Answer: I remember texting someone for about three days that I was dating yet no response. She said that she didn't charge her phone, yet every time we were together her phone was always in her hand and she was always using it. I couldn't bring myself to believe her.

3. **If your friends had to describe your dating life in one word, what would that word be?**

Answer: Precarious.

4. **In your opinion, has social media sites complicated the dating world, helped it or a little bit of both?**

Answer: Both. Complicated it to where if females see you have photos with other females on your social network page, they assume you're a player. I've discovered that going out with female friends is really what helps you get a date.

5. **Have you ever went to see a movie alone?**

Answer: No I haven't. I need someone with me.

6. **Are you still friends with past lovers or was the entire relationship ruined?**

Answer: I'm cordial with past lovers.

7. Is seven days a week enough days for you or do you need more days, if so how many?

Answer: I need more days, 10 days a week, with no weekends.

8. If you had more time what would you do with it, how would you use it?

Answer: More time to travel and network.

9. How many hours of sleep do you get in a night?

Answer: Four and a half but I'd like to get at least seven.

10. How do you feel about texting?

Answer: I'm a master texter.

11. If you were given an extra million dollars today, what is the first thing you'd buy with it or use it for?

Answer: Get together with a few producer and actor friends of mine to produce a movie.

12. What do you think are some of the key ingredients to a successful relationship or marriage?

Answer: Honesty, being unpredictable, attraction, creativity and being physically fit.

13. What do you think are some of the key ingredients to being successful in life and in business?

Answer: Being ambitious, driven, open minded, social and a forward thinker.

14. Are you Single By Choice or Single By Necessity?

Answer: I'm single and looking.

DAY 31
AGREE TO DISAGREE.

One of the hardest things I had to learn as a single professional was how to compromise. When you're accustomed to being in charge of everything and you only have you to answer to, you expect to get what you want, when you want it, however you want it, as much as you want it, all the time, and for the most part, I got exactly that. But as life progresses, different people enter your circle and you encounter new experiences, you soon realize that there may be times when you can't find mutual ground in a situation. Relationships alone will test your ability to be fair, and if you're wise enough to reflect and be taught by certain situations that transpire, you'll learn a thing or two for the better. I wish this was the case for all people, even myself. The world would be a much happier place if so.

There will come a significant day, a monumental minute during a specific hour, a unique space of human existence carved out especially for you and another person where you'll have to learn to agree to disagree. That was not easy for me to write just now. It took me much longer to reach this place of understanding in life. I've always wanted to be understood, have the last word and make sure my way was the best way, but now I know better, and I'm more successful because of this awareness. I'll say this, if you ever find someone who agrees with everything you do, say, pursue, like and dislike, don't do and never has an opinion about any of it, get away from that person because they may not be altogether truthful. Even I would like to know how another feels regarding a particular subject or situation, even when it's totally opposite of the way I do. Whether you agree with them or not, listening to opinions from others can still be a valuable asset to your growth and mental expansion.

Don't expect your family, friends, significant other, co-workers, employees or your employer to agree with everything or anything you say, do or believe. We were all raised and brought up differently, have diverse or contrasting backgrounds, some having offbeat perceptions, so it wouldn't make sense to think your point of view alone is the only accurate one. Instead, we must focus on listening and truly understanding the other person. It's their job to do the same towards you. Once that is established mutually, there is nothing left to do or decide upon. You can definitely try to find some middle ground to agree on but there's no guarantee you will. Respect one another and decide to agree to disagree while understanding how each individual feels. This may sound minuscule but if it hasn't happened to you yet, it will, and when it does, use this information I'm giving you. It can save your job, your relationship, your friendship, your marriage and even your life. Some people are crazy, they really are, so just agree to disagree and keep the peace. You never know what people are capable of these days, so don't give anyone a reason to show you.

DAY 32
WHAT ABOUT YOUR FRIENDS?

It's true, you become what you surround yourself with. It amazes me how so many people are unconsciously aware of this, even after decades of being alive, many of us still don't get it. Most single people have single friends, most married couples have friends that are also married or in a relationship, and of course the same goes for business and career, most successful people have successful friends. Entrepreneurs will likely have more friends that are entrepreneurs than those that work for others. Friends are a pivotal part of life, they remind us of where we come from and some remind us of what we don't want to return to. In the single life, friends can be your greatest asset, especially if it's taking you quite some time to find a special someone. I wouldn't recommend a single friend to give the best advice on being in a relationship though, however some singles do have more experience than those that are attached. I always believe, at the end of the day, going to a profitable source, those who are or have been successful at doing what you desire, these people are the best resources for information. Better safe than sorry, find a couple that has weathered every storm for advice, sometimes our friends can't see any further than we can.

You better believe business professionals need an even more thorough evaluation when selecting friends, why, because money is on the line, reputation, public image and influence come into play. The 'He say, She say' won't have any say-so, you need all facts when it comes to your career and success. Ironically, everyone wants to be their own boss yet few really have the dedication, discipline, commitment and discernment to run a successful business long-term. It takes great instinct and timing to be a success in anything. Your circle of friends, or contacts, or colleagues, whichever you decide to label them, all play some role in what you accomplish as far as your level of focus, distractions and encouragement. Are they pushing you to become greater, adding value to your visions and ideas, or are they constantly distracting you and draining your time and energy to where you've slacked off from getting things done? Beware of those with too much free time. Annually evaluate your friends on a personal and professional level. Being single, you don't have the benefit of sharing your thoughts, concerns, ideas and so on with someone special everyday, so you have to rely on quality friends to make that happen. Don't feel bad when some disappear as your life expands, not everyone is capable of moving up the ladder with you. Real friends will want to grow with you. Your success should only encourage and inspire them to seek their own.

DAY 33
I KNOW WHAT YOU DID LAST YEAR.

The past is tricky. It can be one of our greatest allies or our biggest enemy. Everyone has a past, some are bright and some are completely dark. No matter what your past consists of, it's what we take from the past and how we apply it to our future that counts. Most people would rather forget past relationships that didn't work out. Others wish they could revisit or resume theirs. As long as we learn something and grow from every past experience, then we're on the right path. Whether you were in the wrong or in the right, your overall perception of the experience, no matter how painful, will determine your next level of understanding in life. Understanding the purpose of past experiences and their role in the future grants access to wisdom.

If you were mistreated or heartbroken, were you able to truly forgive? Did the experience make you more aware of the type of person or people you truly need in your life? Which mistake can you admit to on your part that you won't repeat in the future? Looking back should always serve as teaching. It's the same with your business or professional life, we constantly use the past to enhance and guide our future, so we should do the same in our personal life as well. The ultimate purpose of the past is to show you how to take your life to the next level every year. This can only be done by observation of not only the faults and mistakes of others, but more so taking yours into account as well, then seeking to become greater. Therein lies true success and understanding, blaming no one, but thanking everyone for the past experiences that were divinely orchestrated to make you a better person.

DAY 34
ONLY STOP TO CHANGE DIRECTIONS.

Bad breakups, losing a job, closing a business, having to make an unwanted career change, hard financial times, all of these can make anyone feel like giving up. Life will pitch so many curve balls and can deliver numerous sharp turns until it makes you want to stop, throw in the towel and retreat. As determined as we are as business professionals, we too have moments where we ask ourselves "Is it all worth it?" Sometimes it can be even harder for the single professional, especially if you're used to having someone special in your life to lean on, confide in and to make you feel better. Well no matter what you go through or come across in life, none of it is worth giving up on yourself. Life is too short to let something that doesn't kill you slow you down. There is indeed a healing process but heal as you continue.

Losing a loved one or a close friend, that's a different situation, and whatever you have to do to deal or mourn properly is fine, but outside of that type of hardship, you must maintain a relentless spirit to fight the good fight of faith and stay on course. That's why it's important to seek out your passions, skills, gifts, talents and interests, so you'll always know what you can turn to as a reserve if something else folds or doesn't work out career wise. When dealing with relationships and people, keep in mind that we're all incapable of getting everything right and we're all imperfect. With this at the forefront of my mind, it helps me deal with my biggest disappointments involving people, so that I can keep things moving right along.

DAY 35
DON'T GET UPSET. GET BACK TO LIFE.

On any given day something or someone could make you upset. For a lot of us, this happens more than we'd like, for some almost everyday, so now would be a good time to learn how to deal with unscheduled anger. There are those people who flip out instantly while others let situations come to a boil over time. I've known friends, family and colleagues that couldn't find a happy moment in anything on a daily basis, except clocking out from work or going to bed. Bitterness and unhappiness will cause you to get upset even when great things happen for you, which is really odd if you ask me. I've come to a place where I now realize that each day is truly a gift. Your life or another life can be taken away in the next breath, so why spend hours, an entire day, a week, upset or angry over something that you can't go back and change. I'm not sure if it's a maturity issue or an awareness issue, maybe it's both. I used to get upset over the smallest thing in the past, I was being a brat, I can admit that now.

After expressing how you feel about a situation, the next best thing to do is to channel whatever anger or resentment or attitude you still have into something more positive and productive, that's what I do. It took me a while, years, OK I'll be honest, my entire life up until now, to get to this place of understanding. Back in the day I'd rather just curse you out and send you on your way, out of my life. Now that I've matured, been through almost all circumstances known to man and grown in wisdom, I now know that redirecting negative emotions and feelings into something more positive, is the healthiest and most progressive thing you could ever do in this life of uncertainty. No one was born with the responsibility of making you feel good or bad. You are ultimately responsible for how you allow others to influence the way you feel. So instead of fighting, having four year disagreements and not speaking to one another, or having social media battles or beef online, how about you go exercise, read a book, volunteer to help the less fortunate, do something that really matters. We get too caught up in situations during our life, when instead we should be getting caught up in producing better situations for our life.

DAY 36
36 HOURS A DAY. 8 DAYS A WEEK.

I need more time, I can't deny it. No matter how much I plan things out, I still need more time. Do you face this same dilemma as a business professional? As a human being? I'm for certain if there were at least thirty-six hours in the day and eight days in a week I'd have it all together, I'm sure, maybe. For some reason I think I'd need even more hours and days after a while. If you're anything like me or a serial entrepreneur, then you try to get as much done as possible each day and you stay on the lookout for the next great opportunity. Sometimes I get so carried away until I lose track of time and the days of the week. I've missed a few Wednesdays and Thursdays, finding out from friends and associates that the day was now Friday or

Sunday. It happens. There has to be a balance though, especially if we want to maintain sanity and keep up with the days of the week.

The power of discipline, mixed with determination, organization and great decision making, allows you to accomplish far more than most people. It doesn't matter what you're pursuing, as long as there's a master plan set in place, everything will be possible. Take for example, millions of people say they want to write a book but how many actually accomplish it or even start writing? The majority answer is zero. I have to put myself on the most outrageous and unimaginable schedules around the clock to finish books, launch marketing campaigns, produce events, other tasks, to stay ahead of the game and to stay in somewhat decent health during the process. It's not easy and definitely not popular but it's the only way you'll be able to meet certain deadlines. Maybe we really don't need more time, maybe we just need to omit some of the non-beneficial and time-consuming things that aren't aiding us in accomplishing our immediate goals. That's a thought. It sure does free up my time to do what needs to be done. What can you omit or do without daily so that you can spend more time on fulfilling your dreams and your life mission?

DAY 37
THE ALL-NIGHTER.

Just when you thought this book was safe, well it is. I know that title raised a few eyebrows but there are many types of all-nighters we can experience. I remember when I'd meet someone of interest, before I realized the importance of sleep, we'd stay on the telephone until at least 3, 4 or 5am every night. The conversation went something like "What are you doing? What are you thinking about?", which was repeated every hour, and that was about it. Those were the good 'ole days. Some of us were even lucky enough to actually spend time with that person, in person, watching television or just hanging out, letting time slip right by unknowingly while engulfed in each other so intensely, not realizing that the sun would rise soon.

Business is no exception to all-nighters. Any

determined business professional or business owner will tell you that. All-nighters come with the territory, they are a part of the job description baby, you're either born to do it or born to admire those who achieve great things from it. I remember when I first got the idea for my event company Germaine Moody Events, I honestly stayed up almost thirty-six hours building a website (not having a clue as to what I was doing, that's why it took thirty-six hours), creating event ideas and researching locations to host the events. If it wasn't for my body almost collapsing, I would have been up working even longer or until an ambulance arrived. When the heart knows what it wants, it ignores all restrictions of time and oftentimes health.

Whether it's personal or business, anything you truly desire to achieve from within, be it companionship, a feeling of accomplishment or whatever the case, it will cost you an investment of time. Some, maybe more time than others. The goal is to make sure that what you're contributing your all-nighters to is worth all night and furthermore, worth your life. People waste more time than time itself but even if you've had your share of wasted time, the true testament and power of time is always 'Now'. So take this time, Now, and give your time to what matters, to who matters. Use your time to enhance your life and it will ultimately expand the lives of those around you.

DAY 38
THE POWER OF AN HEIR.

Not all hoping-to-be, soon-to-be or current parents think in terms of an "heir" when they decide to have children, but there are those, especially business professionals, entrepreneurs and public leaders who strategically plan for them, 'heirs' that is. Those of us who are creating or have created brands, businesses, estates, empires and so on often want our children to be an extension of what we have established in our lives personally and professionally. Though I don't believe any parent should pressure their kids to follow their footsteps, I do believe we should aim to provide them with as many options, guarantees and open doors as possible. I know several single professionals who have adopted children with the thought of an heir in mind. There's nothing more powerful than your legacy being carried on and remembered through your children, those who you care about most. Whether it's your traditions, a life of philanthropy, books, music, cherished art or a family business, an heir keeps you relevant and everything you stood for, achieved and worked so hard for. It also gives your children added purpose for their own life, especially if you leave a legacy of philanthropy that continues to help change the lives of others. That should always be carried on to the next generation.

DAY 39
SHARING THE KNOWLEDGE.

One of the benefits of being single and successful is that we may often have extra time to do things like mentor the youth, volunteer, start a blog, write a book or consult someone who needs advice. To me success is only true success when you're able to use your success to make someone else a success. This means giving back, sharing what you've learned, your business experience, your past relationship experiences, your life experiences, the good and the bad. The more people I meet, the more I realize that none of us have all the answers, some have no answers at all but I won't call any names. The best way to get all the answers is to know a lot of smart and wise people, that's why networking is so important, which is simply sharing resources and knowledge. Your life should always expand when you network. It's our responsibility to be there to assist others in doing the same down the line. It's a domino effect and it makes you invaluable, which can turn into unlimited opportunities, access, influence and truly immeasurable success. Your expertise, your insight, your knowledge, your advice, your wisdom, was all a gift to you that was divinely meant to give away to those coming after you.

DAY 40
THE POWER OF SUCCESS.

As our forty-day journey comes to a close, I hope that I was able to bring some joy, awareness, guidance and a little bit of laughter into your life. I'm grateful that you made time to get a copy of this book and took even more time to read it. What you hold in your hand is the prime example of my final devotion topic, The Power of Success. Successful people are the most influential people. The world listens to and follows the successful. Doesn't matter if you're single or coupled, race doesn't play a role, nor does gender or sexual orientation have any say so anymore. All it requires these days to have followers is that you are a success. Influence creates the followers, those that admire you, support you and some will even die for you. Followers give you power and at that point, you have to decide on how to use that power, not just for yourself, but for those around you and maybe even the world.

After releasing my book "50 Seeds of Greatness", which included 357 business professionals from 106 countries, it gave me great global influence, which turned into followers, then into power. Power to use my present and soon to be unlimited connections and contacts to help me develop, produce, market or launch any new projects, books or ventures around the world almost instantly. With the influence I had already obtained from our international networking events, I gathered those 357 professionals to do something that has never been done on that scale with the written word, and that was to use the world to inspire the world. Each and every person in the book has witnessed their own level of success, so joining forces only increased our influence and now people everywhere are benefiting from the inspiration, motivation and encouragement we all created together in "50 Seeds of Greatness".

Whether it's business, your career, helping others or a vision you have, pursue it with tenacity, do it 1000% because 100% will not compete in today's market. The world itself has become lazy and gotten comfortable with convenience. Technology has enabled us to have a lot of cool gadgets in this current era, in addition to getting work done faster and gathering information in little to no time, but it has also introduced a new generation of complacent, uncertain, distracted and lazy followers who desire not to think, create, communicate or work for themselves. Knowing this, we must live with a plan and strategy even more, every single day. The world watches the successful, the lens is always on them. The world is the microscope, success is the specimen.

If you have social success, being connected to a lot of people, use your influence to gather people together to stand up for injustice or to raise money for the less fortunate in times of crisis and tragedy. If you have financial success, use some of your money to assist in the costs to help bring medical aid those who need it most, like non-profits, food missions and on the ground organizations that really make a difference for people in unfortunate circumstances. Though single, though successful and if your life is anything like most of us, sometimes sleepy, we are the new married, the new family, the new leaders, and it must become our mission, whether we're single for the rest of our lives or coupled, to make sure our lives mean more to someone else than just ourselves. That is true success. OK, time for a power nap. Be brave friends and rock the world!

More books by Germaine Moody

The Quotes

Discover Wisdom
100 Days of Inspiration and Power.

50 Seeds of Greatness

An Abundance of Person
You were created from genius and born to greatness.

Upcoming books by Germaine Moody

The Networking Bible
Access to your greatest Influence, Wealth and Power.

The Power of Dance

The Power of An Entrepreneur

www.ingramcontent.com/pod-product-compliance
Lightning Source LLC
LaVergne TN
LVHW051122080426
835510LV00018B/2175